PARENTING

A HANDBOOK WITH IDEAS
FOR DOING YOUR BEST

Savannah M. Young and Susan B. Philpott

Bloomington, IN  Milton Keynes, UK

authorHOUSE®

AuthorHouse™
1663 Liberty Drive, Suite 200
Bloomington, IN 47403
www.authorhouse.com
Phone: 1-800-839-8640

AuthorHouse™ UK Ltd.
500 Avebury Boulevard
Central Milton Keynes, MK9 2BE
www.authorhouse.co.uk
Phone: 08001974150

First published by AuthorHouse 6/19/2009

ISBN: 978-1-4259-8807-4 (sc)

Printed in the United States of America
Bloomington, Indiana

This book is printed on acid-free paper.

Dedication

Our book is dedicated to all the parents and school principals and teachers who love, care, and have high hopes for children.

Acknowledgments

This book is our personal statement based on our years of experience as parents and teachers. The thought, energy, and passion put forth in this book come from the love, hope, and concern we have for children.

We are indebted to our families and friends who supported and guided us to the completion of this endeavor. We are most grateful to Pat Whitener for her encouragement and understanding of what we want to share with parents. Our thanks to Aline Phillips who some time ago reviewed our first draft and thought it worth reading on her journey as a parent. We want to express our gratitude to Armand Gilbert and Helen Herndon for their help with computer technology, proofreading, and editing.

About the Authors

Savannah Miller Young
Ph.D. St. Louis University

Savannah is the Assistant Superintendent of Elementary Education in the Ferguson-Florissant School District (Missouri), after serving thirty-nine years as a teacher, principal and district administrator with the St. Louis Public Schools. Savannah has taught at all grade levels, working with children and their parents to help them build strong relationships at home, in school, and in life. Savannah's husband, now deceased, was a retired educator. She has two stepchildren and six grandchildren.

Susan B. Philpott
B.A. Wellesley College

Susie has taught Adult Literacy and English as a Second Language. She is a reading tutor for elementary school children and volunteers with Reading Is Fundamental in the St. Louis Public Schools. Susie is married to a physician. She has three children and five grandchildren.

Table of Contents

PREFACE

It cannot be stressed enough that parents contribute to society by raising children to be literate, responsible, disciplined, and law-abiding citizens. The positive impact of good parenting on society is immeasurable.

As parents, you enter uncharted territory when a child enters your life. And like most parents, when you interact with your children, you rely on recordings in your mind of how your parents interacted with you. You use the good recordings and sometimes, unfortunately, the bad or unpleasant ones as well.

PARENTING provides simple suggestions about how to show love, to teach, to protect, to discipline, and to encourage children to be the best that they can be. We urge parents to use this handbook as a guide for adopting new methods and ideas for building parenting skills in order to break negative parenting styles.

Did you know that parents help change the world for the better just by being attentive and loving to their children? We hope this handbook will provide guidance as you work toward being the outstanding parent you want to be. Some pages will provide space for you to record your thoughts. As you do, think about what effect your parenting style has on your child or children.

Because we want our work to be gender neutral and want to give equal recognition to girls and boys, we have chosen to use the pronouns he/his/him and she/her interchangeably.

Along with space for you to **Record Your Thoughts**, this handbook includes practical suggestions for family interaction in **Parent and Child Connections.**

Before you start reading, think about your mother and father's parenting styles and then record your thoughts.

Record Your Thoughts

What examples of your mother and father's parenting styles do you continue to carry in your mind?

Good Examples

_____

_____

_____

_____

_____

_____

_____

Bad/Unpleasant Examples

_____

_____

_____

_____

_____

_____

_____

What being a parent means.

Naming Your Child

As a parent, be thoughtful and careful when naming your child. The name you give your child is your first gift to that child. Consider if the name you choose is appropriate for a youngster as well as for an adult.

William Shakespeare said, "What's in a name?" Much! Your child's name can give your child confidence, make socializing easy, and promote courage to face challenges or aspire to leadership.

Some considerations when choosing your child's name:

- Be sure to find out what the name means and what other words may be associated with that name.

- It is not advisable to make up names and be careful about combining names. Your child needs a name that is clear to others.

- A child's name should be easy to pronounce and spell so your child will not have to keep explaining it to others.

- For ease of pronunciation, avoid selecting a first name that ends with the same sound that begins the last name.

- Consider how your child's name will sound when she is called from across the classroom or playground.

- Your child's name should not refer to anything that is negative, silly, controversial, or divisive.

- If the child's initials spell a word, be sure it is a positive word and not one with a negative or offensive connotation.

- Think about nicknames and how the name you choose can be turned into a nickname your child will resent.

After all:

- You are the MOST important person in your child's life.

- You are your child's FIRST teacher.

- You want the BEST for your child.

- You can and WILL MEET the challenges of good parenting.

- You can HELP your child to be a lifelong learner.

> **Becoming socialized and learning to read are the two major goals to be achieved in childhood.**

Number 1: Becoming Socialized

Good manners, respecting differences in others, taking turns, and playing fair enable a child to become socialized. A child who learns these skills will be respected and valued in return, setting the tone for a positive life journey.

Number 2: Learning to Read (and Write)

The importance of your role in helping your child learn to read is well documented. Learning to read and mastering reading skills is greatly influenced by the spoken language ability a child has developed. Both Betty Hart (1995) and Betty Bardige (2006), in their books <u>Meaningful Differences</u> and <u>At a Loss for Words</u>, emphasize that language development beginning at birth through age 5 is paramount for success in school and life.

Learning to read is enhanced when you:

- ◆ Talk to and listen to your child.
- ◆ Read to your child.
- ◆ Teach your child advanced words and concepts.

Record Your Thoughts

What do you do to help your child achieve these goals?

_____

_____

_____

_____

_____

_____

_____

_____

_____

_____

_____

_____

_____

> ## The basic ingredients for good parenting are love, love, and more love.

Love is found in and expressed by demonstrating:

- ☐ a positive attitude
- ☐ compassion and patience
- ☐ wisdom and understanding
- ☐ justice and firmness
- ☐ hard work and responsibility
- ☐ honesty and fair discipline
- ☐ self-control
- ☐ fortitude
- ☐ gratitude and generosity
- ☐ humility and forgiveness
- ☐ integrity and respect
- ☐ attentiveness
- ☐ active listening
- ☐ understanding and empathy
- ☐ sympathy

Record Your Thoughts

What makes your parenting special?

❑_____

❑_____

❑_____

❑_____

❑_____

❑_____

❑_____

❑_____

❑_____

❑_____

❑_____

❑_____

❑_____

❑_____

❑_____

❑_____

Your child needs to feel loved, accepted, valued, and connected.

♥ Show your love by hugging, touching, smiling, laughing.

♥ Tell your child that you love…love…love and value him.

♥ Give your child a sense of belonging by involving her with family, friends, neighbors, a place of worship, and a community.

♥ Your child's best protection from getting into trouble (drugs, gangs, sex, illegal behavior) is a strong relationship and connection to parents and family that he can count on.

Record Your Thoughts

How do you show love and acceptance to your child?

_____

_____

_____

_____

Your children need your presence more than your presents.
– Jesse Jackson

Parent and Child Connections

✔ Say "**I LOVE YOU**" to your child at least once every day.

✔ Give special names to displays of affection ("Bear Hugs," "High Fives," "Butterfly Kisses," etc.).

✔ Give your child a brief talk every day about your expectations for her success at home and at school.

✔ Tell your child how you learned to be the good person you are today.

It's not only children who grow. Parents do too. As much as we watch to see what our children do with their lives, they are watching us to see what we do with ours. —Joyce Maynard

Your child needs to be able to trust you.

	YES	SOMETIMES	NO
When you make a promise, do you keep it?			
If you lie, are you aware that lying creates mistrust?			
Do you apologize when you make a mistake?			
Do you admit when you are wrong?			
Do you forgive honest mistakes of others?			
When your child admits committing wrongful acts, do you thank him for his honesty?			
When talking to your child, do you use profanity, racial slurs, or other unkind words?			
Do you show respect to others, including relatives, neighbors, the school principal, and teachers?			

Record Your Thoughts

What do you do to make your child trust you?

❑ _____

❑ _____

❑ _____

❑ _____

❑ _____

❑ _____

❑ _____

❑ _____

❑ _____

❑ _____

❑ _____

❑ _____

❑ _____

❑ _____

❑ _____

❑ _____

Your child needs to be able to rely on you.

Give extra support to your child during stressful times such as moving, divorce, family member's illness or death, financial troubles.

Help your children to get along with each other. Sibling rivalry and children fighting with each other are common in many households. Parents can help their children by:

- Making sure each child knows she is valued and has a distinct place in the family.

- Giving each of your children special attention.

- Making sure each child has his own belongings, friends, special events, and parents' time.

Be sensitive to a child's difficulties in adjusting to separate households, stepparents and blended families. Clarify the rules of the different households.

A child's birth order can have an effect on how she sees herself and how she sees herself in relation to her siblings. We are all familiar with how middle children are expected to act. Here are some of the "said to be" typical behaviors of children by birth order: "only" children are spoiled, the first child is controlling, the second child looks for attention, the middle child of three feels left out and alone, and the youngest child expects others to wait on him. Be wary of presupposing that your child will fit these expectations, but be alert to the family dynamics which often do occur.

Parents of an "only" child should teach him to share, respect, and care about others. In addition, parents should be mindful of letting the child enjoy being a child, while also encouraging him to be the best he can be.

Single parents are in some ways the ultimate parents. They have it all and have it all by themselves. Being a single parent means having to perform the duties of two parents. If you are a single parent, you can maximize your parenting efforts by involving your children in family meetings, family time and family routines with a household schedule outlining specific times for meals, homework, chores, and social activities, including watching TV. Be sure to take time with your child.

Develop a network of supportive relatives, neighbors, and friends.

Single parents should be cautious about how they handle their own personal relationships, especially sexual. Often children feel abandoned when their parent's friend is perceived as playing the role of a spouse.

Be familiar with helpful community agencies. Seek professional help from the school or a social service agency if you feel your child cannot cope with anger or stress, abuses drugs or alcohol, displays violent or antisocial behavior, seems depressed, or has sudden changes in behavior, appetite, or sleep patterns.

Be aware that neglect and abuse may hinder brain development in children. **The following actions are considered child abuse:**

- Beating, hitting, jerking, snatching, twisting, pinching, choking, or shaking.

- Taping your child's mouth shut or forcing soap into your child's mouth.

- Threatening bizarre punishment (locking in a closet, putting in the toilet or into the garbage, or leaving in a car).

- Harsh scolding for accidents (bed-wetting, spilling, getting dirty) or for making a low grade in school.

- Failing to provide adequate food, shelter, clothing, or supervision.

How kids look and what they wear are part of fashion and clothing fads that are involved in growing up. But your child needs your guidance and support when he is selecting clothing and deciding what to wear. Do all you can to make sure your child does not overindulge in the latest fads.

For girls, insist that they dress appropriately for their age. Little girls dressing as grown-ups can put them at risk. Make sure they do not wear clothing that is too tight, too short, too low cut or exposes any body part inappropriately.

For boys, do not permit their clothing to be too big and their pants too low. Help them to practice tucking in their shirts, and insist that school clothing be clean and tidy. You should apply the same standard for inappropriate exposure.

Pay attention to your child's school's dress code. Listed below are some examples of what many schools and colleges consider inappropriate dress:

- Any article of clothing displaying obscene or inappropriate printing.

- Tops that are too revealing, that display bare midriff or cleavage.

- Clothing which sags. The waistband of pants, shorts, skirts, or jeans must be secured at or above the waist.

- Any clothing which shows underwear or undergarments.

- Clothing, jewelry, emblems, badges, symbols, or signs which are designed to show gang membership or affiliation. (*A "gang" is defined as any group of two or more persons whose purposes are the commission of illegal acts.*)

- Shirts and blouses are expected to be TUCKED in at the waist.

- Extremely short skirts or shorts are not to be worn.

- Appropriate footwear must be worn at all times. Students are not to wear house shoes, have bare feet or wear socks without shoes.

The following items are not to be worn without adequate cover:

- Tube tops, spaghetti straps, tank tops (if the shoulder straps are less than three fingers wide), cut-offs, midriff shirts/blouses, muscle shirts.

- Tights or spandex.

- See-through clothing (including, but not limited to tops, sleeves, legs, and backs).

Record Your Thoughts

How does your child show that he needs emotional support?

_____

_____

_____

_____

Are you able to ask "open questions"? Examples: _Is there something going on that you wanted to tell me about? How can I help you? You seem sad/upset/ stressed._
What have you found that you can say to your child to encourage him to open up? _____

_____

_____

_____

_____

_____

_____

Are you able to listen to your child without making judgments, jumping to conclusions, or making light of her concerns?

_____

_____

_____

_____

_____

How do you show you are interested and listening?

_____

_____

_____

_____

_____

Children want to make their parents happy.

Discipline is teaching children how to gain control of their emotions and behavior. Children want to be disciplined.

Discipline lets your children know you care about their well-being and expect them to be and do their best.

Discipline should not make children feel bad about themselves. It should be used to give guidance.

Give your child guidelines so she will know what is expected of her.

Be patient with your child. Children have short attention spans and can become frustrated if they are not having success or if the task is too hard.

Teach your child to set goals. Help your child to think positively about achieving goals. Make suggestions to help your child reach those goals. Illustrate to your child how you set and achieve goals.

Some Goals to Set

Goal: Get up in time to eat breakfast before school or plan to have breakfast at school. How? Set an alarm clock.

Goal: Get enough sleep. How? Go to bed nine hours before you need to get up.

Goal: Finish homework every night. How? Do homework as soon as you get home from school.

Record Your Thoughts

What does your child do to gain your approval? Have you recognized his effort? How do you acknowledge his effort?

_____

_____

_____

_____

_____

_____

_____

_____

_____

_____

_____

Your child learns attitudes, beliefs, behavior, manners, and language at home.

Respect is an attitude. Respect is not only given to people who respect you, but is given to everybody. Respect makes life easier at home, at school, and everywhere else.

Teach your child to respect others. Teach your child to use respectful language and gestures such as holding a door open for others.

Teach your child to be proud of herself, while at the same time being respectful and tolerant of those who are of a different race, culture, ethnicity, gender, age, economic status, ability, or talent.

A child who feels good about himself will be less likely to dislike those who are different.

If you are accepting of others, your child will copy your attitude and behavior.

Be the model for your child to demonstrate patience, a positive attitude, and a sense of humor.

Laugh more than you frown.

By your own actions teach honesty, self-control, generosity, tolerance, kindness, helpfulness and fairness. Be a good "role model".

Teach good manners by using them yourself. Manners are about being kind, thoughtful, appreciative, and caring about others.

Don't ever use or allow profanity or offensive language.

No name-calling. Be respectful of your child and insist on respect from her.

Your child learns how to handle conflict and solve problems from watching you and seeing how you handle and solve problems.

Record Your Thoughts

Among all the character traits to be learned, respect is paramount. Do you consider yourself to be respectful?

_____

_____

_____

_____

_____

_____

_____

_____

How do you teach your child respect?

Parent and Child Connections

Say *please, excuse me,* and *thank you* to your child.

Make a "Cuss Jar." Anybody in the house who uses bad language must put a coin in it. When the jar is full, buy a book or a game.

Make a "Good Manners" chart. Give the child a star each time he does something polite.

Help her write "Thank You" notes for a gift or an invitation she has received.

Role-play situations with your child to demonstrate how to handle conflicts, take turns, and follow directions.

Talk with your child about honesty and the importance of being honest.

Keep a scrapbook of your child's accomplishments.

Good manners to share with your child:

√ Look at the person you are talking to.
√ Use her name: "Hello, Ms. Jones."
√ Hold the door open for adults and people who need help.
√ Speak clearly so others can understand you.
√ Shake hands when you are introduced to someone. Use a firm grip.

Don't worry that children never listen to you; worry that they are always watching you. —Robert Fulghum

> # Your child needs self-confidence in order to trust, to be hopeful, to be purposeful, and to be responsible.

Respect your child's feelings, individuality, and privacy.

Respect your child's opinions; listen and be understanding.

Encourage him to use words to describe how he feels.

Praise him far, far more than you criticize.

Encourage her efforts. Don't ridicule, raise your voice or "put her down" in front of others.

Forgive mistakes.

Parent and Child Connections

Say "thank you" to your child if he does something kind, helpful, generous, or respectful.

Pay your child a compliment every day.

Some examples of compliments:

- I like the way you fixed your hair.
- You worked hard last night and got all that homework done.
- You really helped by playing with your little brother for so long. He had fun with you.
- It's great that you got the trash out in time for the pickup.

Record Your Thoughts

What are you usually like around your child? Positive?
Negative? Unpredictable?_____
_____
_____

In what ways do you find that your child's behavior
mirrors yours? _____
_____
_____

Do you have or do you display behaviors you would like
to change or modify in order to be a better role model
for your child? _____
_____
_____

Have you noticed a difference in your child's behavior
when he is complimented or thanked?_____
Describe this behavior._____
_____
_____
_____
_____
_____
_____
_____
_____
_____
_____

Your child needs and deserves to understand your rules.

Be consistent in your expectations of your child.

Set boundaries and clear limits.

When possible, give your child some choices when making the rules. Let her help in setting the daily routine.

Be consistent and fair in enforcing limits. If you don't follow through, your child will soon learn that you don't really mean what you say.

Set consequences that your child will experience if he doesn't follow the rules.

Be realistic about what your child is able to do. Don't expect more from her than she can manage.

Reward a good attitude and good behavior.

Parent and Child Connections

Give "smiley stickers" to an obedient child. Use the words *obey* and *obedient*.

Post written reminders about "The Rules". That way you don't have to always boss or nag your child.

Record Your Thoughts

List the basic rules of your household that you hold your child responsible for following:

_____

_____

_____

_____

What are some rewards you can give for following the rules?

_____

_____

_____

_____

_____

_____

_____

Your child needs to learn self-discipline and responsibility.

Give your child a chance to make choices. Give her responsibilities so she can feel capable and independent.

Encourage your child to learn new skills and allow him to make small mistakes he can learn from.

Help your child handle anger, stress, and conflict without using violence.

Help your child learn how to think ahead and to delay gratification by exercising self-control.

Teach your child about setting short- and long-term goals.

Avoid giving your child more than he needs. Parents who "over-buy" risk spoiling their child. Encourage him to save some of his earnings or allowance.

Teach money management to your child by talking about making choices. Assign him some items to select when you grocery shop. Let your child do comparative shopping with you. Help your child learn how to make a budget.

Parent and Child Connections

Make a "Job List" together. Use stars for good work.

Obtain a piggy bank so your child can start saving.

Open a bank savings account for an older child.

Record Your Thoughts

What are your child's responsibilities?

_____

_____

_____

_____

_____

How do you expect your child to show self-discipline?

_____

_____

_____

_____

_____

If you want your children to keep their feet on the ground, put some responsibility on their shoulders. – Abigail Van Buren

Discipline your child with love.

It's OK to let your child know when you are angry and why you are angry. Anger is a normal emotion. But wait until you are in control of your anger before disciplining your child.

Use polite words. Don't call your child dumb, lazy, stupid, worthless, irresponsible, good-for-nothing, ugly, or a liar.

Tell your child what you expect. Give reasons for your expectations.

Avoid lecturing. Do not scream, yell, or hit because it will not solve the problem, and worst of all, your child will imitate your behavior.

Give "time outs" and encourage your child to talk about what caused him to break the rules and what he could have done differently.

If punishment is needed, let the child help decide on the consequences (grounding or limiting activities, taking away privileges, or giving additional chores).

Make the punishment "fit" the offense.

Praise your child for regaining control.

Remember that a child's bad behavior is often because he cannot express his anger or emotions with words or self-controlled behavior.

Pick your battles. You can and should ignore some things.

Record Your Thoughts

How will your child know that you are expressing love when you discipline?

_____

_____

_____

_____

_____

_____

_____

_____

_____

_____

_____

_____

_____

Should you spare the rod and spoil your child?

To SPANK or not to SPANK???

How do you feel about spanking?

Did your parents spank you?

If you do spank, for what kind of misbehavior do you use this form of discipline?

- Spanking teaches that violence can be used to solve problems.
- Spanking tells your child you are out of control.
- Spanking can become abusive and cause physical harm.
- Spanking can cause children to fear and resent their parents.
- As children grow older, spanking does not work.

But if you, as a parent, feel that spanking is necessary in certain circumstances, then:

⊗ Never **spank** when you are angry. **NEVER!**

⊗ **Spank** only for clearly established bad behavior.

⊗ If you **spank,** never use anything but your hand.

⊗ Never **spank** hard enough to cause physical harm. **NEVER!**

<u>**Record Your Thoughts**</u>

How do you usually discipline your child? What consequences do you give your child for inappropriate behavior?

_____

_____

_____

_____

_____

_____

What would you like to change about how you discipline your child?

_____

_____

_____

_____

_____

_____

Alternatives to Spanking

√ Giving time out

   How and where will you give time out?

_____

√ Withholding possessions

   What possessions will you withhold?

_____

√ Restricting fun activities

   What fun activities will you restrict?

_____

√ Restricting socializing

   What socializing activities could you restrict?

_____

√ Having a stern conversation

   What will you say during the stern conversation?

_____

√ Increasing opportunities to do chores

   What additional chores will you give?

_____

<u>Record Your Thoughts</u>

What will you do to avoid spanking your child?

_____

_____

_____

_____

_____

_____

_____

_____

_____

_____

_____

Each day of our lives we make deposits in the memory banks of our children.
—Charles Swindoll

Be positive when dealing with bad behavior.

Tantrums are a normal part of development and indicate that the child is out of control. Wait it out and don't give in. Don't shake or hit the child.

When the **tantrum** is over, ask the child to explain the problem in his own words. Insist that your child use his words to explain needs, concerns, and differences.

Hitting your child encourages the behavior you are trying to stop. If your child is under three years, simply tell him *no,* distract, and redirect him. Children older than this should be told to *use their words,* not their fists. **Hitting** and **fighting** are inappropriate behaviors. The idea that if someone hits you, you should hit him back, is a bad idea. Children should be instructed to seek help from adults: parents, relatives, teachers, neighbors or other adults.

Lying can often be prevented by the way you question your child. If you know she played hooky from school, don't say, *did you go to school today?* because she'll probably lie to avoid punishment. Instead say, *I found out you skipped school today. Let's talk about what's going on.* This approach will make your child more comfortable telling the truth because you are willing to listen and pay attention to her. Parents would do well not to use the words *lie* or *lying* with their children. Parents can use phrases such as: *being honest,* or *please be up front with me,* or *just tell me all of it, from beginning to end.* The words *lie* and *lying* are mean, harsh words.

Children often fabricate and embellish what they have to say in order to get attention and gain approval of friends and parents. When your children tell the truth, praise them and let them know how grateful you are for their honesty. When chastising your child, do not make dishonesty the main issue. If you do, your child will simply tell you what she thinks you want to hear, rather than own up to her misbehavior.

Stealing is a common problem many children engage in while growing up. Children younger than four do not understand the meaning of ownership and do not know it is wrong to take things that are not theirs. Even so, when young children take something that does not belong to them, they should be instructed to return it and be told what stealing means.

By the time children reach five, they should know it is wrong to take things that belong to others and doing so is stealing. Children steal for many reasons - for example, having a lack of self-control, to feel empowered, to gain status among peers, to get attention, and to show a lack of respect. Help your child to feel secure and appreciated by giving him positive attention and demonstrating how much you value and love him.

Some Examples of Parents Giving Positive Attention:

√ Spending time together
√ Giving hugs
√ Telling him "I love you"
√ Sharing your life stories
√ Giving special gifts
√ Going shopping
√ Going on an outing

__Record Your Thoughts__

Does your child, at times, manipulate or control you?
_____If so, what does she do to assert control?

_____

_____

_____

_____

_____

_____

How do you respond?

_____

_____

_____

_____

_____

_____

Are you pleased with the outcomes?

_____

_____

_____

_____

_____

_____

How do you respond to your child when he does
something praiseworthy?

_____

_____

_____

_____

_____

_____

A child should never be compared to other children.

Accept and appreciate your child as she is.

Verbalize your pride in your child.

Don't tell him you wish he were more like somebody else.

Encourage her in the things she does well rather than focusing on her failures or mistakes.

Parent and Child Connections

Play "Today's Best Thing about (child's name)" every morning. This can be anything from noticing his happy smile to complimenting her on the fact that she cleaned her room.

Play a game with her that she can play well. Be sure she wins sometimes. This helps her feel successful in your eyes.

Look at his photographs with him from the time he was a baby up to the present. Point out how cute he was and how (handsome, smart, etc.) he is now.

Talk about something she did that made you feel proud of her because she was brave/kind/helpful/strong/etc.

Record Your Thoughts

In what ways do you reinforce your child's sense of self-worth?

_____

_____

_____

_____

_____

_____

_____

_____

_____

_____

_____

_____

Your child needs attention and mental stimulation.

A child's success in school is directly related to how much an adult talks to and plays with the child.

Talk and sing to your child from birth onward so he learns language skills. Words are the food of the brain.

Your child needs to hear many, many words.

Read...read...read to your child. Play games, do yard and household jobs together and talk all the while.

Discuss with your child about being smart and how important school is to help him learn and become smart. Make sure he understands that "smart" does not apply just to certain races, nationalities or ethnic groups and that anyone can be smart, especially him. Emphasize that smartness comes as a result of how hard you work.

Be sure she spends more time interacting with you and others than watching TV or playing video games. In fact, you should have a Home TV Watching Policy that permits TV watching only after all homework has been finished. Limiting your child's opportunities to watch TV will be a positive decision that will pay off for your child, you, and your family.

Encourage your child to be involved in school, community, or faith-based volunteer projects.

Keep your child intellectually stimulated with conversation.

Parent and Child Connections

- Read a story to your child every night before bedtime. This is a good time for cuddling and talking.

- Use toys and puppets to play talking games.

- Cook something together that your child likes to eat. This is a good time to teach measurements.

- Play a word game or card game together.

- Visit the public library, the zoo, or a museum.

- Let your child help you open the mail, plan a meal or a family party.

- Take your child with you to the grocery store or to the mall. Talk about making choices and comparing costs.

- Encourage new interests and hobbies (collecting rocks, stamps, or baseball cards).

- Help curiosity and interest to blossom in your child by pointing out and talking to your child about what interests you, such as weather, the shapes of clouds, kinds of cars, buildings, plants, and animals. Your curiosity will rub off on your child.

- Read the newspaper comics or Kid's Activities together.

- If you have a household chore to do let your child help you by folding laundry, dusting, straightening papers, or drying dishes.

- Look through old family photos together— especially pictures of her as a baby.

- Let him help you collect clothes that no longer fit the family members. Take him along when you donate them to your church bazaar, the Salvation Army, the Goodwill, or other local charitable organization.

Record Your Thoughts

In what ways do you reinforce your child's sense of self-worth?

_____

_____

_____

_____

_____

_____

_____

_____

_____

_____

_____

Learning is for life.

Remember that you are your child's first teacher. Model the joy of learning by pursuing new skills and interests you enjoy. Stay interested in your own academic development and learning.

Get to know and understand your child's personality, academic strengths, and how he learns.

Make sure your child has a comfortable, stimulating, and well-lit home learning environment. Your child will need learning supplies that include: pencils, paper, books, magazines, encyclopedia, a dictionary, and a thesaurus.

Make sure your child is involved in many learning experiences. You and your child should take outings to the zoo, museum, botanical gardens, supermarkets, art galleries, department stores, and relatives' homes.

Take time every day to teach your child lessons of love and hope.

Make sure your child does her homework. Always help your child if she asks you to check her homework. Quiz your child on spelling or listen to her read or tell a story.

You can help your child be a good learner by fostering and supporting:

- Self-esteem (feels secure and knows love)
- Responsibility (helps out at home)
- Self-confidence (works well with others, makes reasonably sound choices easily, and uses good manners)
- Self-acceptance (can admit mistakes, apologize, share, take turns and be a good sport)

Record Your Thoughts

What do you do to help your child experience happiness and joy?

_____

_____

_____

_____

_____

_____

Kids spell love, T-I-M-E. - John Crudele

> # School is different from home. In life outside of your home, your child will face new ideas, social pressures, and different rules.

Teach your child rules for being part of a group.

Teach your child how to play fair in order to exercise good sportsmanship.

Teach your child to take correction and criticism with a positive attitude and behavior.

Make sure your child knows it is OK to lose sometimes.

Make sure your child develops a balance between sports and academics.

Have high expectations for your child's academic and sports performance.

Help your child to do his best and to have fun when participating in school and sports activities.

Attend sports events, school outings and parent nights.

You are your child's role model – be respectful to all the adults who work in your child's school.

Remind your child to say thank you to neighbors, friends or relatives who do favors for him, give him a ride home or buy him a treat.

Talk with your child about how to avoid joining in if a friend suggests doing something she knows is not acceptable in your family.

If your child is invited to a friend's house, explain to him that other people's homes, food, or habits may be different from yours.

Record Your Thoughts

What kind of person do you want your child to be?

_____

_____

_____

_____

_____

_____

_____

_____

_____

_____

> **Not respecting other people's human rights is characteristic of bullying and criminal behavior. Bullies hurt others on purpose.**

<u>Teach your child not to be a bully.</u> This means being a role model yourself by being tolerant of others and not taking advantage or showing your anger when things do not go your way.

Children learn powerful lessons of self-control and tolerance from watching how their parents and relatives handle adversity and solve problems. Your calm, kind demeanor and consideration of others set the tone for your child's behavior.

Some children become bullies because they are permitted to have their way, often getting away with inappropriate behavior.

Parental help and support are most important to ensure that children are tolerant of others who are different because of race, religion or sexual preference. If you think your child is a bully, talk to your child, to his teacher, and to other adults with whom your child has social interactions.

<u>Teach your child how to respond to bullies.</u> Bullying behavior is seen when children tease, play the dozens (mama talk), signify (to insult or put down), ridicule, curse, fight, or exclude others. Your child should immediately report bullies to you, to the teacher, and to the school principal or other adults.

The United States Department of Health and Human Services identifies the following signs in the behavior of children who are victims of bullying:

- ❏ Not wanting to attend school, ride the bus, or participate in school activities.

- ❏ Sad, moody, or depressed after school.

- ❏ School performance declining.

- ❏ Trouble sleeping, frequent bad dreams or nightmares.

- ❏ Inability to make friends.

- ❏ Loss of appetite.

- ❏ Being anxious and having low self-esteem.

- ❏ Making negative comments about their personal skills and ability.

- ❏ School materials and clothing are taken or destroyed.

- ❏ Has physical altercations, often getting cuts and bruises.

- ❏ Displays aggressive behavior.

Talk with your child's school principal about how the school handles bullies and bullying and how you can work with the school to eliminate bullying.

Good parents help their children want to learn.

Talk to your child from the day she is born because learning to talk is the first step to learning to read. Talk about everything, ask questions, explain events, and tell stories.

Give your child praise...and more praise...and MORE PRAISE.

Display his drawings and schoolwork at home.

Teach your child to listen. Give clear directions and be sure she can understand and follow directions.

Read newspaper articles about national, world, and political conflicts, including war and violence. Ask your child for her ideas on how to solve problems. Share your ideas with your child.

Teach a sense of time:

- Being "on time" and completing a task in the time allotted

- Knowing days of the week, months, hours, minutes

- Using a calendar to mark birthdays, holidays

Create a daily routine with definite times for:

- Three (3) nourishing meals

- Homework and home chores

- Reading together

- Family time

- Daily hygiene: brushing teeth, bathing and shampooing, brushing, combing or braiding hair. (Remember, do not braid your child's hair too tightly, especially the "baby hair" around the front, sides, and back. When hair is braided too tightly it breaks off or comes out, and often does not grow back.)

- Going to bed for 8 to 10 hours of sleep. (A tired child cannot learn.)

Record Your Thoughts

Our Family's Schedule

_____

_____

_____

_____

_____

_____

_____

_____

_____

_____

_____

_____

_____

_____

_____

Learning at school starts at home.

Home is where one starts from. – T.S. Elliott

When parents are involved in their children's education at home, the children do better in school.

Read to your child. A child who knows how to read and loves books will be a lifetime learner.

Reading to your child helps her expand her vocabulary, understand new ideas, learn about other people and the world she lives in. Your child will discover that books are a source of pleasure as well as information.

Always speak in complete sentences and insist that your child speak in complete sentences. Monitor your child's pronunciation and enunciation of words such as: **that**, **this**, **them**, **those** and word endings such as: **-s, -t, -ed, -ing**.

Help your child to value the language he speaks at home, but at the same time learn to speak Standard English. Speaking Standard English will make it easier for your child to learn to read, to write, and to spell correctly.

Make sure your child knows what words mean and how they relate to other words. Spend time using words to make sentences and to develop stories. Request speech and hearing screening if you notice:

- ✓ **Adults outside the family can't recognize most of his words.**
- ✓ **Your child doesn't seem to understand others.**
- ✓ **Your child's sentences don't make sense.**
- ✓ **Your child can't express what he is thinking.**
- ✓ **Your child consistently seems to ignore you when you speak to her.**

Parent and Child Connections

- Share your own childhood memories and funny stories about school, friends, and teachers.

- Show your child photos of yourself doing things when you were her age.

- Start a home library.

- Obtain a library card for your child and go to the library on a weekly basis to borrow books.

- Encourage writing a journal, writing letters, drawing, and coloring.

- Read aloud with your child every day.

- Show your enthusiasm for your child's reading efforts.

- After reading a story to your child, ask him to tell you the story in his own words. This kind of activity will clarify your child's comprehension.

- Ask your child questions about the story, such as: What happened? Why do you think it happened? Who or what caused it to happen? What do think will happen next?

- Play word games that include helping your child to develop word and concept knowledge.

This means helping your child learn many words and concepts to ensure she has a well-developed vocabulary. You can start by being sure your child has mastered word and concept knowledge related to her daily life.

Word Knowledge and Concept Development

Directions: Play a word game with your child to develop and improve his vocabulary by teaching him to relate words and concepts that are familiar to him. Choose a concept, an idea or a theme such as **time,** and ask your child to identify as many words as possible that come to mind when he thinks of the concept of **time.**

Words Related to the Concept of Time

day	week	month	noon	morning
minute	second	clock	timekeeper	supper
dinner	year	decade	century	watch
summer	autumn	spring	season	brunch
fall	winter	semester	breakfast	lunch

Words Related to the Concept of Mall

stores	enclosed	restaurant	elevator	shopping
decoration	security	coffee shop	large	plants
people	shops	fountains	building	restrooms
cafes	clothes	movies	games	children
food	services	jewelry	post office	escalator

Words Related to the Concept of Weather

sunshine	rain	pressure	air	storm
snow	clouds	wind	breeze	hail
sleet	chill factor	freeze	temperature	wind chill
warm	hot	drizzle	forecast	meteorology
cool	dry	vane	blowing	thermometer

Other Examples of Concepts

animals	plants	tools	sizes	play
body parts	toys	sports	playground	wealth
clothes	shapes	love	family	library
colors	numbers	seasons	school	recreation
self	peace	space	earth	travel
foods	poverty	music	sky	beauty
furniture	symbols	art	technology	neighbor
buildings	careers	exercise	friendship	helpers
computer	entertain	feelings	talk	beliefs

In addition to language and reading readiness, your child should be involved in at-home learning experiences in the <u>arts, physical development, health, science, social studies,</u> and <u>mathematics</u>.

For you, this means providing guidance and support for your child to have purposeful, meaningful, and rigorous at-home learning experiences.

Record Your Thoughts

What activities can you do at home to promote learning?

Mathematics _____

_____

_____

Science _____

_____

_____

Writing _____

_____

_____

Social Studies _____

_____

_____

Spelling _____

_____

_____

Art _____

_____

_____

Music _____

_____

_____

Physical Education (movement) _____

_____

_____

Health _____

_____

_____

_____

_____

Handwriting _____

_____

_____

_____

Help your child adjust to school.

Show your respect for the school as a positive place to learn.

Respect for school is first shown by making sure your child goes to school on time every day. School attendance is closely tied to school achievement.

Do not criticize the school's rules or its staff in front of your child.

Have high expectations for your child's school performance.

Help your child prepare for all of the tests he will take at school.

If your child is making low grades, talk with her teacher about how you can help your child improve her performance.

Participate in all school activities:
- Join the PTO, PTA or Mothers' Club.
- Attend parent conferences.
- Serve as a Room Parent.
- Communicate with the school regularly.
- Regularly read the school's website.
- Read all school notices, even the ones you do not have to sign.
- Ask teachers to keep you informed of your child's progress or problems.
- Find out if your employer donates to schools or gives time off for parents to participate in school events.
- Vote in all school board elections.

Engage your child in experiences outside home (faith-based school, camp, library, scouts, Little League sports, and supervised after-school programs). Being involved in these kinds of activities will help your child adjust to school.

Record Your Thoughts

What are your child's activities outside of school?

_____

_____

_____

_____

_____

Are there other or new activities that you want to plan for your child's participation?

_____

_____

_____

_____

_____

_____

Make sure your child does homework.

With your child, make a set of homework rules.

Make sure your child knows and understands your household's homework rules. In the rules identify:

- Time to start: Begin as soon as your child comes home from school.

- Time spent: Every day after school, your child should spend at least an hour doing homework and thinking about school. Of course, the time will vary for elementary, middle, and high school youngsters.

- Place: Identify a place in your home, i.e., the kitchen or dining room table.

- Climate: While completing homework, ensure quiet - no video games, TV, radio, visitors, texting, or phone calls.

- Confirmation: Either or both parents should review and sign the homework.

- Supplies: Be sure your child has all the necessary supplies at home to do school work (paper, pencils, pens, construction paper, erasers, markers, crayons, rulers, pencil sharpener, scissors, tape, paper clips, hole puncher, stapler, index cards, folders for reports, calculator, age and grade-appropriate encyclopedia, dictionary, thesaurus, magazines and newspapers). Use internet websites to help your child with homework.

Record Your Thoughts

What concerns do you have about your child's school?
Plan a meeting with the school principal and your
child's teacher to discuss your concerns. Take some
notes.

_____

_____

_____

_____

Are you pleased with the outcomes?

_____

_____

_____

_____

Start planning early for your child's future.

Begin talking with your child early in elementary school about college and preparing for going to college.

Make sure your child learns to read and masters reading comprehension by the end of the third grade. After third grade, continue the academic support in middle and high school with strict home/school rules and tutoring (if necessary).

Do all you can to have a computer available to your child.

Be sure your child, at every grade, does all the assigned homework, develops good study habits, and uses time well.

Talk with your child's teacher and school counselor to make sure he is taking challenging courses and has a college preparatory curriculum.

Make sure your child has advanced intellectual experiences such as beginning algebraic thought as early as kindergarten, begins a foreign language in elementary school, and takes advanced courses in middle and high school.

Get involved in all school activities such as Parent Nights, school visits, and parent conferences.

Attend College Fairs with your middle and high school students.

Record Your Thoughts

What are you doing to make sure your child will be able to attend college?

_____

_____

What is the focus of your child's kindergarten through grade twelve academic program?

- college preparatory
- military service
- vocational training
- other

_____

_____

_____

What financial plans are you making to take care of your child's education beyond high school?

_____

_____

_____

_____

Your child needs to be kept safe and healthy.

Accidents are the most common cause of death for children from birth to age 14, exceeding death from diseases, drugs, or violence.

Show your child how to cross streets, and point out the **danger** of running out between parked cars.

Teach school **bus safety**: stay seated, never run to or from the bus, wait until the driver sees you and signals all-clear before crossing the street.

Teach daily good **health habits**: brush teeth, wash hands often, bathe regularly, get enough sleep, eat a nutritious breakfast, avoid junk food.

Childhood **obesity** has become a national health problem. Teach your child to make nutritious choices, limit portions, cut down on fats, eat fruits and vegetables, and get at least one hour of exercise daily.

Encourage **outdoor** activities, exercise, playing, and socializing.

Plan many **family outings**; take walks in the park, trips to the museum, zoo, theater, or library.

Children should wear **helmets** when riding a motorcycle, bicycle, tricycle, scooter, or a skateboard. One out of seven children age 14 and under have suffered head injuries in bicycle accidents. Helmets help prevent serious injury.

Your child's **bike** should be the right size, not too large or too small. The child should be able to straddle the bicycle while keeping both feet on the ground.

When children ride bicycles, they should know to ride
defensively where they can be clearly seen by motorists and
others. Be sure the children wear their helmets.

Limit all television watching, and monitor the programs your
child sees. Talk with your child about what he is watching.

When your child uses a **computer**, an adult should monitor
its use. If your child uses the internet, teach your child
about protecting her identity. Don't allow access to "adult-
oriented" web sites.

Discuss the dangers of **alcohol**, **drugs**, and **smoking**.

Discuss the risks of **sexual activity**. Talk with your daughter
and son about abstinence from sexual behavior in order
to prevent unplanned pregnancy and to be protected from
contracting sexually transmitted diseases. Teach your own
values, but education about sexuality should start early at
home.

Keep any **guns** in locked boxes out of children's sight and
reach. Store ammunition separately from guns. Start at an
early age to teach your child never to touch a real gun.

Teach **"Home Alone" safety rules**. Be sure your child is old
enough to understand the rules, can obey directions, and
can use the telephone before leaving him alone.

Insist on use of **car safety seats or seat belts**. State laws
require that car seats be used for children weighing less
than 40 pounds. Booster seats should be used for children
weighing between 40-80 pounds.

Child-proof your house when children start crawling and
walking.

Get regular medical and dental **check-ups** for your child. Keep immunizations up to date. Follow instructions for prescribed medications.

Purchase medicine with **child-resistant caps** that you keep tightly closed and in a safe place.

Educate yourself about the dangers of **lead poisoning** from peeling, flaking, or sanding old house paint. Have your child's blood tested for lead at an early age. Lead poisoning can cause learning and neurological problems.

<u>Keep all poisons out of reach</u>. Post the Poison-Control number near your phone. Keep doctor-recommended information on hand in case the doctor tells you to make your child vomit.

If a child gets burned, contact your doctor. Remove clothing from burned area. Do not apply butter or other ointment. Do not use ice, but run cool water over the burned area for about 5 minutes. In cases of severe burn over a large area, call 911 or go to the emergency room.

Install smoke detectors and change the batteries twice a year.

Never leave a small child alone in the car, tub, or pool.

If your child runs a **high fever**, follow your doctor's recommendations, or you can bathe or sponge her in tepid (barely cool) water. Do not use cold water or alcohol.

Watch for **choking** hazards such as buttons, coins, small toys/ toy parts, balloon pieces, nuts, popcorn, hard candies. Learn the Heimlich maneuver.

Parent and Child Connections

- Teach your child her first and last name, address, telephone number and your name and work telephone number.

- Tell your child about other trusted adults he can go to if you are not available. Be sure your child knows how to reach them.

- Be sure your child can use the telephone to call 911 in case of an emergency .

- Role-play what your child should do if approached by a stranger, is touched by someone inappropriately, or is threatened.

- Teach your son or daughter to say "NO", to RUN AWAY and to TELL a trusted adult if anybody touches or asks to touch his or her private parts.

- Practice safety skills (crossing streets, fire, tornado, earthquake, etc.).

- Teach your child safety tips to use around pets and other animals.

- Your phone is your "Help Connection". Make sure it is always in working order. Consider giving your responsible preteen or teenager a cell phone to keep in touch with you and to use in emergencies.

Record Your Thoughts

What are your special safety rules?

_____

_____

_____

_____

In case of an emergency what is your Emergency Plan?

_____

_____

_____

_____

Do all your family members know what to do?_____
Where will they go?_____

_____

_____

Emergency telephone numbers

FIRE_____

_____

POLICE_____

_____

_____

Where are the emergency numbers and the emergency
plan posted in your home?

_____

_____

Make a list of helpful telephone numbers.

Helpful numbers can be found in local telephone directories. The emergency numbers are often found on pages bordered in color in the middle of the white pages directory.

SERVICES	TELEPHONE NUMBER
Adoption	
Alcohol and Drug Information	
Birth Certificates	
Bus and Transportation	
Community Services	
Child Abuse and Neglect Hotline	
Child Health Insurance	
Consumer Hotline	
Crime Victims	
Disabilities	
Domestic Violence Hotline	
Equal Employment Opportunity	
Family and Children's Services	
Health Department	

Hospital/Clinic	
Hunger Hotline	
Immigration Services	
Law Enforcement	
Lead Poisoning	
Legal Services	
Mental Health Services	
Parent Stress Hotline	
Parks and Recreation	
Rape Crisis Hotline	
Rat Control	
Safe Schools Hotline	
Senior Citizen Services	
Suicide Prevention	
Venereal Disease and AIDS	
Voter Registration	
Weather	

OTHER PHONE NUMBERS	

EDUCATIONAL WEBSITES

TITLE	URL	DESCRIPTION
CHILD DEVELOPMENT		
Early Childhood Educators' and Family Web Corner	http://users.sgi.net/ ~cokids/	Best meta-site on early childhood development
Early Childhood Today	http://teacher.scholastic. com/products/ect.htm	Activity plans, nutritional information
I Am Your Child	http://www.iamyourchild. org/	Information for parents on child development
Idea Box	http://www.theideabox. com/	Early childhood ideas: activity, season, games, music and songs, recipes, and crafts.
Little Explorer Picture Dictionary	http://www. enchantedlearning.com/ Dictionary.html	This dictionary is great for young children
Sesame Workshop	http://www. ctw.org/	Games for the preschooler featuring the beloved Sesame Street characters

EARLY CHILDHOOD		
Activity Idea Place	http://www. 123child.com	Activities for young children
BBC Parenting	http://www. bbc.co.uk/ parenting/your_kids/	Parenting section: child and school, preparing for nursery or elementary school, and developmental stages
ChildFun.com	http://www. childfun.com/ themes/school.shtml	Kindergarten readiness checklist, helping your child become a better reader, and a very informative Ask the Teacher section
Gayle's Preschool Rainbow	http://www. preschoolrainbow.org/	Activity ideas
Getting Young Children Ready to Learn	http://www. humsci. auburn.edu/parent/ready/ paus1.htm	How to get students ready to learn by developing language abilities, self-control, social skills
LANGUAGE ARTS		
Children's Literature Web Guide	http://www. ucalgary.ca/ ~dkbrown	This is one of the best websites there is: book award winners, teaching ideas.

Cool Word of the Day	http://www. edu.yorku.ca/wotd	Child vocabulary enrichment: a "cool" word of the day
KidBibs	http://www. kidbibs.com	A teaching and parenting resource site designed to support children's reading, writing, and learning.
Poetry on KidzPage	http://www. veeceet.com/	An eclectic mix of poems, including students' submissions
READING FIRST		
Helping Your Child Become a Reader	http://www. ed.gov/pubsparents/Reader/index.html	Activities teachers and parents can use to get children to become readers and get excited about language and learning
Education Place's Reading/Language Arts Center	http://www. eduplace.com/rdg/	Collaborative reading projects developed by teachers
Home for the Holidays... Reading Together	http://www.ed.gov/inits/holidays/index.html	Tips for parents on reading well with their children
Preventing Reading Difficulties in Young Children	http://stills.nap.edu/html/prdyc/	Identifies the predictors of reading difficulties

Reading is Fundamental	http://www. rif.org	Interactive and motivating activities for kids of all ages and their families
Ready to Read*Ready to Learn	http://www. ed.gov/inits/ rrrl/index.html	Laura Bush's Educational Initiatives: Bring What Works to Parents; The Tools to Teach What Works; Strong Teachers, Strong Families, Strong Students
Starting Out Right	http:/bob.nap.edu/ readingroom/books/sor/	Methods for growing up to read from birth to age four and methods for preventing reading difficulties

Record Your Thoughts

What websites do you plan to focus on the most?

TITLE	URL	DESCRIPTION

Notes: